SCHOLASTIC

Let's Find Out
My REBUS Reader

I0890034

Evergreen Leaves Are Always Green

by Amanda Miller

SCHOLASTIC INC.
New York Toronto London Auckland Sydney New Delhi Hong Kong

In winter, some trees have lost all of their .

leaves

But an evergreen's  are always green.

leaves

An evergreen’s  leaves are always green.
But you may see red  berries.

An evergreen's  leaves are always green.
But you may see white  snow.

An evergreen's  leaves are always green.

But you may see brown  pinecones.

An evergreen's  leaves are always green.

But you may see **colorful**  lights.

Look at Evergreen Leaves

Evergreen leaves can be different shapes and sizes.
But they are always green!

spruce

longleaf pine

fir

holly